SUMMER MATH WORKBOOK

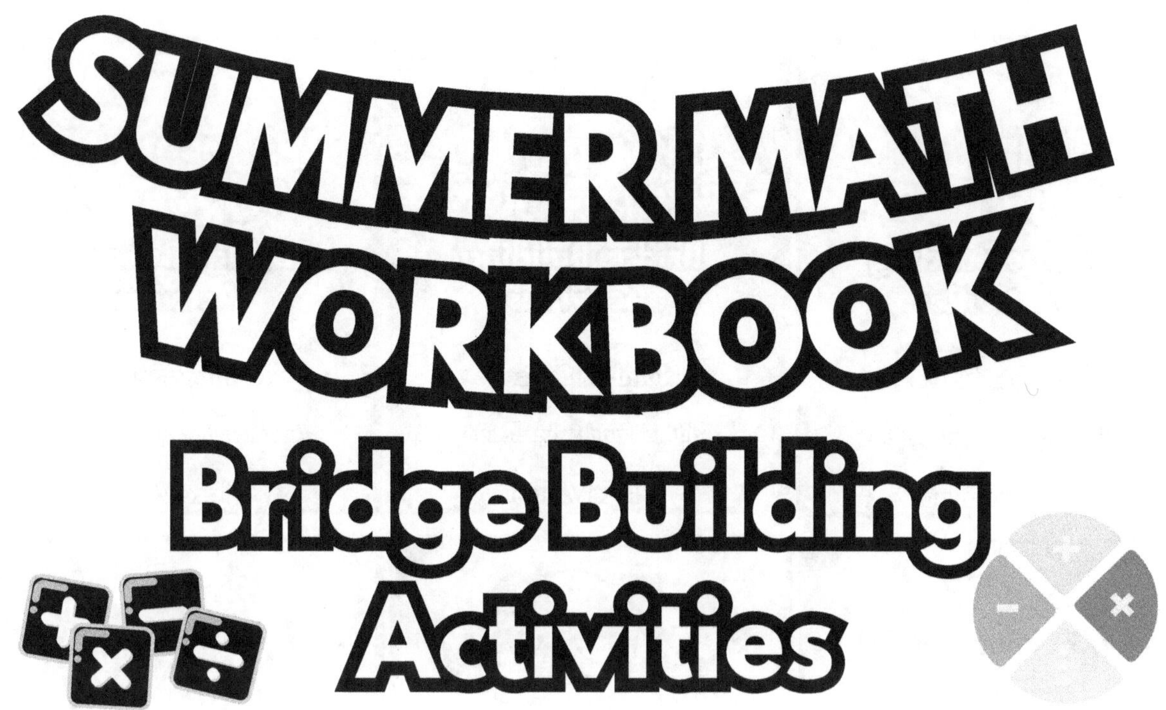

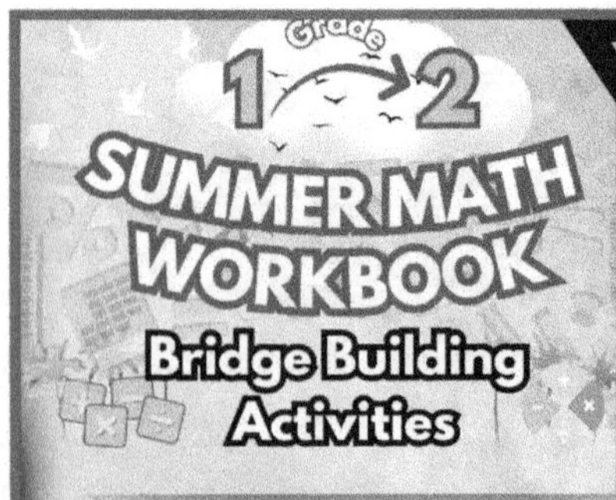

Grade
1 → 2
SUMMER MATH
WORKBOOK
Bridge Building
Activities

Number Sense

Addition and Subtraction

Place Value

Grade
2 → 3
SUMMER MATH
WORKBOOK
Bridge Building
Activities

Number Sense

Addition and Subtraction

Place Value

Grade
3 → 4
SUMMER MATH
WORKBOOK
Bridge Building
Activities

Number Sense

Addition and Subtraction

Place Value

Grade
4 → 5
SUMMER MATH
WORKBOOK
Bridge Building
Activities

Multiplication and Division

Place Value and Units

Fractions and Geometry

Grade
5 → 6
SUMMER MATH
WORKBOOK
Bridge Building
Activities

Multiplication and Division

Factors and Multiples

Fractions and Geometry

Grade
6 → 7
SUMMER MATH
WORKBOOK
Bridge Building
Activities

Arithmetic

Algebra

Geometry and Statistics

Grade
7 → 8
SUMMER MATH
WORKBOOK
Bridge Building
Activities

Ratio and Percentage

Algebra and Cartesian Plane

Geometry and Statistics

Grade
8 → 9
SUMMER MATH
WORKBOOK
Bridge Building
Activities

Ratio and Percentage

Algebra

Geometry and Graphing

Grade
9 → 10
SUMMER MATH
WORKBOOK
Bridge Building
Activities

Factoring and Distributing

Algebra

Geometry and Graphing

Introduction

As parents and educators, we understand the pivotal role that mathematics plays in shaping a child's academic journey and future success. Yet, the path to mathematical proficiency can often seem daunting, filled with challenges and complexities. That's where the transformative power of Summer Bridge Building Activities books comes into play, illuminating the way forward with clarity, precision, and purpose.

Summer vacation is a time for rest and relaxation, but it also presents the risk of the "summer slide," where students lose some of the academic gains they made during the school year. Summer Bridge Building Activities books are specifically designed to tackle this challenge, ensuring that your child stays academically engaged and prepared for the upcoming school year. These books provide a seamless bridge from one grade to the next, reinforcing essential skills and introducing new concepts that will give your child a head start.

Imagine your child eagerly diving into the pages of a Summer Bridge Building Activities book, greeted by clear, engaging content that demystifies complex mathematical concepts. With each turn of the pages, they embark on a journey of discovery, encountering thoughtfully curated practice questions that reinforce learning and sharpen problem-solving skills. As they unveil the answers to those questions, a sense of accomplishment blossoms within them — a tangible reward for their hard work and dedication.

Summer Bridge Building Activities books transcend traditional educational tools; they are meticulously crafted to build a deep and enduring understanding of mathematics. These books follow a sequential and logical progression, starting from fundamental principles and advancing to sophisticated problem-solving strategies. Each chapter is designed to build on the previous one, ensuring a solid and comprehensive foundation for future learning.

Parents, we yearn for nothing more than to see our children thrive academically and personally. We want to witness the spark of inspiration ignited within them as they overcome academic challenges with confidence and poise. Summer Bridge Building Activities books serve as indispensable partners in this noble endeavor, offering not just practice questions but the keys to unlocking a world of academic and personal opportunities.

Visualize the pride on your child's face as they master a challenging math concept, the joy they experience when their efforts yield results, and the confidence they gain with each success. These pages are designed to make learning math a positive, enriching, and deeply rewarding experience that will benefit them throughout their academic journey and beyond.

For educators, Summer Bridge Building Activities books are invaluable allies in the quest to cultivate mathematical proficiency in the classroom. Accompanied by comprehensive guides and readily available answers, instructors can focus on mentoring and nurturing their students, secure in the knowledge that these books provide a robust framework for effective learning.

Within the pages of Summer Bridge Building Activities books lies not just the promise of academic excellence, but the seeds of a brighter future. By integrating these resources into your child's summer routine, you are bestowing upon them the gifts of confidence, curiosity, and a lifelong love of learning.

Invest in your child's future today with Summer Bridge Building Activities books — because every great journey begins with a single step, and this step can change everything. Keep the momentum of learning alive over the summer, and watch your child soar to new academic heights.

Contents

Exponents	1
Square and Cube Roots	4
Multiple Operations with Fractions	7
Order of Operations (PEMDAS)	11
Mixed Numbers	16
Equations (One Side)	22
Solving Inequalities	27
Evaluate Equations	35
Percentage	40
Percent Word Problems	45
Ratio and Proportion Word Problems	50

Grade
7 - 9
PRE ALGEBRA
WORKBOOK
BRIDGE BUILDING
ACTIVITIES
Equations, Inequalities and Expressions
Linear Equations Graphing and Slope
System of Equations Quadratic Equations

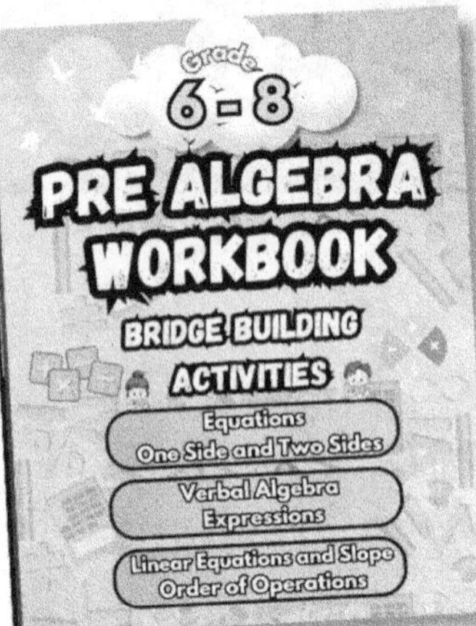
Grade
6 - 8
PRE ALGEBRA
WORKBOOK
BRIDGE BUILDING
ACTIVITIES
Equations One Side and Two Sides
Verbal Algebra Expressions
Linear Equations and Slope Order of Operations

Grade
5 - 6
PRE ALGEBRA
WORKBOOK
BRIDGE BUILDING
ACTIVITIES
Integers, Mixed Numbers Decimals and Fractions
Place Value Exponents and Roots
Percentage and Ratio Word Problems

PRE ALGEBRA
WORKBOOK
for
Beginners
Integers Fractions, Mixed Numbers
Place Value Exponents and Roots
Percentage Ratio Conversion

PRE ALGEBRA
WORKBOOK
for
Adults
Integers Percent and Ratio
Equations, Inequalities Expressions
Order of Operations

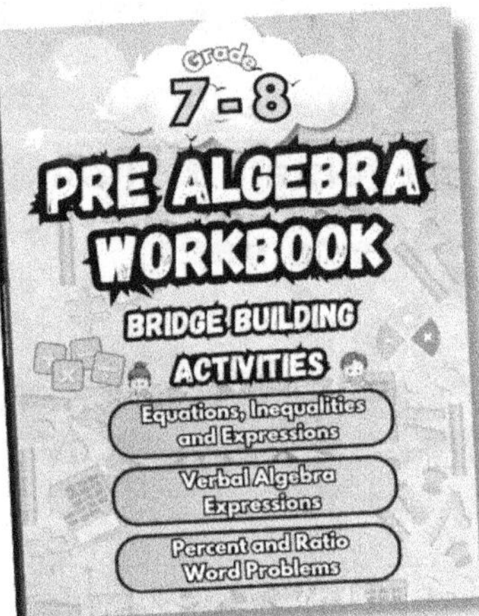
Grade
7 - 8
PRE ALGEBRA
WORKBOOK
BRIDGE BUILDING
ACTIVITIES
Equations, Inequalities and Expressions
Verbal Algebra Expressions
Percent and Ratio Word Problems

Grade
9 - 10
PRE ALGEBRA
WORKBOOK
BRIDGE BUILDING
ACTIVITIES
Equations and Inequalities Verbal Algebra
Linear and Quadratic Equations
System of Equations Polynomials

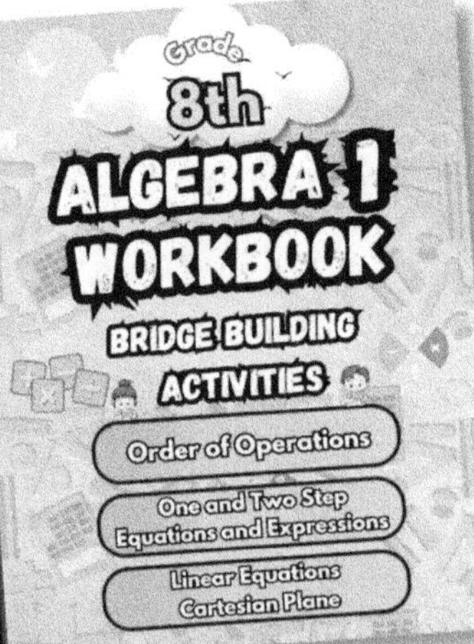
Grade
8th
ALGEBRA 1
WORKBOOK
BRIDGE BUILDING
ACTIVITIES
Order of Operations
One and Two Step Equations and Expressions
Linear Equations Cartesian Plane

Grade
7 - 9
ALGEBRA 1
WORKBOOK
BRIDGE BUILDING
ACTIVITIES
Integers Order of Operations
One and Multi Step Equations and Expressions
Linear, Quadratic Equations Equations One Side, Two Sides

<u>**Exponents**</u>

An exponent tells us how many times a number (called the base) is multiplied by itself. It is written as a superscript to the right of the base number. For example, in 2^3, 2 is the base and 3 is the exponent.

Rules:

1. **Product Rule**: When multiplying powers with the same base, add the exponents.

$$a^m \times a^n = a^{m+n}$$

For example:

$$2^3 = 2 \times 2 \times 2 = 8$$

$$3^2 \times 3^4 = 3^{2+4} = 3^6 = 3 \times 3 \times 3 \times 3 \times 3 \times 3 = 729$$

2. **Quotient Rule**: When dividing powers with the same base, subtract the exponents.

$$a^m \div a^n = a^{m-n}$$

For example:

$$5^3 \div 5^2 = 5^{3-2} = 5^1 = 5$$

3. **Power of a Power Rule**: When raising a power to another power, multiply the exponents.

$$(a^m)^n = a^{mn}$$

For example:

$$(2^2)^3 = 2^{2 \times 3} = 26 = 64$$

4. **Power of a Product Rule**: When raising a product to a power, distribute the power to each factor.

$$(ab)^n = a^n \times b^n$$

For example:

$$(2\times3)^2 = 2^2 \times 3^2 = 4 \times 9 \; = 36$$

5. **Power of a Quotient Rule**: When raising a quotient to a power, distribute the power to the numerator and denominator separately.

$$\left(\frac{a}{b}\right)^n = \frac{a^n}{b^n}$$

For example:

$$\left(\frac{4}{2}\right)^3 = \frac{4^3}{2^3} = \frac{64}{8} = 8$$

6. **Zero Exponent Rule**: Any nonzero number raised to the power of zero equals 11.

$$a^0 = 1$$

For example:

$$7^0 = 1$$

7. **Negative Exponent Rule**: A negative exponent means the reciprocal of the base raised to the positive exponent.

$$a^{-n} = \frac{1}{a^n}$$

For example:

$$2^{-3} = \frac{1}{2^3} = \frac{1}{8}$$

To evaluate expressions with exponents, we can use:

- **Repeated Multiplication**: Perform the multiplication indicated by the exponent.

- **Using the Rules of Exponents**: Apply the appropriate rule to simplify expressions involving exponents.

Square Roots

The square root of a number is a value that, when multiplied by itself, gives the original number. It's denoted by the symbol √.

For example, the square root of 9 is 3 because 3 * 3 = 9.

Cube Roots

The cube root of a number is a value that, when multiplied by itself twice, gives the original number. It's denoted by the symbol $\sqrt[3]{}$.

For example, the cube root of 8 is 2 because 2 * 2 * 2 = 8.

Exponents

Convert the values.

1. $12^{-2} =$ _______________

2. $19^{-2} =$ _______________

3. $15^{4} =$ _______________

4. $17^{2} =$ _______________

5. $3^{-2} =$ _______________

6. $9^{-2} =$ _______________

7. $12^{2} =$ _______________

8. $8^{3} =$ _______________

9. $15^{-3} =$ _______________

10. $5^{2} =$ _______________

11. $7^{-2} =$ _______________________

12. $7^{2} =$ _______________________

13. $10^{2} =$ _______________________

14. $6^{-2} =$ _______________________

15. $4^{3} =$ _______________________

16. $5^{-3} =$ _______________________

17. $14^{4} =$ _______________________

18. $16^{-2} =$ _______________________

19. $20^{2} =$ _______________________

20. $5^{3} =$ _______________________

21. $8^{-2} =$ _______________________

22. $2^{-2} =$ _______________________

23. $20^{-3} =$ _______________

24. $6^{-3} =$ _______________

25. $4^{-3} =$ _______________

26. $11^{-2} =$ _______________

27. $5^{-2} =$ _______________

28. $4^{4} =$ _______________

29. $19^{3} =$ _______________

30. $14^{2} =$ _______________

31. $3^{3} =$ _______________

32. $17^{-3} =$ _______________

33. $3^{2} =$ _______________

34. $18^{-3} =$ _______________

Square and Cube Roots

Calculate the root of each value.

35. $\sqrt[3]{64}$ = _______________

36. $\sqrt[3]{343}$ = _______________

37. $\sqrt{1}$ = _______________

38. $\sqrt[3]{8}$ = _______________

39. $\sqrt[3]{4{,}913}$ = _______________

40. $\sqrt{4}$ = _______________

41. $\sqrt{49}$ = _______________

42. $\sqrt[3]{729}$ = _______________

43. $\sqrt{81}$ = _______________

44. $\sqrt[4]{2{,}401}$ = _______________

45. $\sqrt[3]{4,096} =$ _______________

46. $\sqrt{729} =$ _______________

47. $\sqrt[3]{1,331} =$ _______________

48. $\sqrt[4]{256} =$ _______________

49. $\sqrt[4]{16} =$ _______________

50. $\sqrt[3]{27} =$ _______________

51. $\sqrt{9} =$ _______________

52. $\sqrt[4]{1} =$ _______________

53. $\sqrt[3]{125} =$ _______________

54. $\sqrt[4]{1,296} =$ _______________

55. $\sqrt{289}$ = _______________

56. $\sqrt[3]{2{,}197}$ = _______________

57. $\sqrt[3]{1}$ = _______________

58. $\sqrt{7{,}056}$ = _______________

59. $\sqrt{6{,}889}$ = _______________

60. $\sqrt{900}$ = _______________

61. $\sqrt{4{,}761}$ = _______________

62. $\sqrt[4]{625}$ = _______________

63. $\sqrt[4]{6{,}561}$ = _______________

64. $\sqrt[3]{1{,}000}$ = _______________

<u>**Multiple Operations Fractions**</u>

Fraction multiple operations involve performing multiple arithmetic operations (addition, subtraction, multiplication, division) on fractions.

We follow (PEDMAS that stands for the order of operations in arithmetic) to solve multiple operations Fractions:

1. **Parentheses:** Perform operations inside parentheses first.

2. **Exponents:** Evaluate expressions with exponents or powers.

3. **Multiplication and Division:** Perform multiplication and division from left to right.

4. **Addition and Subtraction:** Perform addition and subtraction from left to right.

For example:

Let's solve the expression: $\frac{3}{4} + \frac{1}{2} \times \frac{2}{3}$

Step 1: Begin by performing the multiplication operation first:

$$= \frac{1 \times 2}{2 \times 4} = \frac{2}{6} = \frac{1}{3}$$

Step 2: Now rewrite the expression with the result of the multiplication:

$$\frac{3}{4} + \frac{1}{3}$$

Step 3: To add fractions, find a common denominator. In this case, the least common multiple (LCM) of 4 and 3 is 12.

Step 4: Rewrite both fractions with the common denominator:

$$\frac{9}{12} + \frac{4}{12}$$

Step 5: Add the numerators together and keep the common denominator:

$$\frac{13}{12} = 1\frac{1}{12}$$

Multiple Operations Fractions

Find the solution.

65. $\dfrac{3}{4} + \dfrac{1}{5} + \dfrac{1}{4} + \dfrac{1}{4} =$

66. $\left(\dfrac{1}{6} + \dfrac{3}{4} \right) \div \dfrac{5}{9} =$

67. $\dfrac{3}{10} + \dfrac{1}{2} + \dfrac{3}{8} =$

68. $\dfrac{1}{2} + \dfrac{1}{7} + \dfrac{1}{4} =$

69. $\dfrac{4}{5} \times \dfrac{1}{4} + \dfrac{1}{2} =$

70. $\left(\dfrac{2}{3} + \dfrac{4}{9}\right) \times \left(\dfrac{1}{4} + \dfrac{1}{7}\right) =$

71. $\dfrac{2}{9} + \dfrac{3}{10} + \dfrac{1}{2} =$

72. $\dfrac{9}{10} \times \dfrac{2}{7} + \dfrac{2}{9} =$

73. $\left(\dfrac{3}{5} + \dfrac{1}{2}\right) \div \dfrac{1}{6} =$

74. $\dfrac{3}{8} + \dfrac{1}{4} + \dfrac{2}{5} + \dfrac{1}{6} =$

75. $\left(\dfrac{3}{10} + \dfrac{1}{3} \right) \div \dfrac{5}{9} =$

76. $\left(\dfrac{2}{3} + \dfrac{1}{6} \right) \times \left(\dfrac{2}{9} + \dfrac{8}{9} \right) =$

77. $\left(\dfrac{1}{6} + \dfrac{1}{6} \right) \times \left(\dfrac{3}{5} + \dfrac{2}{3} \right) =$

78. $\dfrac{1}{6} \times \dfrac{4}{5} + \dfrac{1}{5} =$

79. $\left(\frac{3}{10} + \frac{4}{5}\right) \times \left(\frac{4}{5} + \frac{1}{3}\right) =$

80. $\frac{3}{10} + \frac{5}{6} + \frac{5}{8} + \frac{7}{9} =$

81. $\frac{1}{4} + \frac{7}{10} - \frac{3}{10} =$

82. $\frac{2}{5} \times \frac{1}{3} \times \frac{1}{4} =$

<u>**Order of Operations (PEMDAS)**</u>

The order of operations, often remembered by the acronym PEMDAS, stands for:

- **Parentheses**: Perform operations inside parentheses first.
- **Exponents**: Evaluate exponents (powers and roots) next.
- **Multiplication and Division**: Perform multiplication and division from left to right.
- **Addition and Subtraction:** Perform addition and subtraction from left to right.

The order of operations helps to clarify which operations should be performed first in a mathematical expression to ensure consistent and accurate results.

- **Parentheses**: Evaluate expressions within parentheses first. If there are nested parentheses, start with the innermost ones and work your way out.

  1. Example: $2 \times (3 + 4) = 2 \times 7 = 14$

- **Exponents**: Evaluate expressions with exponents (powers and roots) next.

  1. Example: $2^3 + 4 = 8 + 4 = 12$

- **Multiplication and Division**: Perform multiplication and division from left to right.

  1. Example: $2 \times 3 + 4 = 6 + 4 = 10$

  2. Example: $6 \div 2 \times 3 = 3 \times 3 = 9$

- **Addition and Subtraction**: Perform addition and subtraction from left to right.

  1. Example: $2 + 3 \times 4 = 2 + 12 = 14$

  2. Example: $10 - 4 \div 2 = 10 - 2 = 8$

Order of Operations (PEMDAS)

Evaluate Expressions.

83. $6 \times 7 =$

84. $7 \times 4 + 8 =$

85. $(9 + 8) \times (4 + 10) =$

86. $7 + 6 + 6 =$

87. $2 \times 2 =$

88. $(3 + 6) \times (2 + 10) =$

89. $10 + 1 + 10 =$

90. $2 \times 6 + 4 =$

91. $9 + 1^2 =$

92. $4 \times 4 + 1 =$

93. $(3 + 1)^2 + (1 + 7)^2 =$

94. $5 + 3 + 5 =$

95. $8 + 10 + 2 =$

96. $(4 + 8)^2 =$

97. $(9 + 1)^2 =$

98. $(7^2) \times (3^2) + 9 =$

99. $1 \times 4 + 1 =$

100. $(5^2) \times (3^2) + 8 =$

101. $(5^2) \times (9^2) + 9 =$

102. $4 + 2^2 + 3 + 5^2 =$

103. $8 + 6^2 =$

104. $(5^2) \times (3^2) + 7 =$

105. $(7 + 6) \div 9 =$

106. $7 + 10^2 =$

107. $(9 \times 9) - (3 + 9) =$

108. $(6 + 4) \div 1 =$

109. $(1 \times 10) - (2 + 1) =$

110. $1 + 10 + 3 =$

111. $(7 + 1)^2 + (3 + 7)^2 =$

112. $(9 + 7) \div 9 =$

113. $(4 + 5)(5 + 4) =$

114. $9 \times 3 + 6 =$

115. $5 + 1^2 + 8 + 1^2 =$

116. $(5 + 5)^2 =$

117. $2 + 6 + 10 =$

118. $(10 + 10) \times (6 + 8) =$

119. $4 \times 3 \times 2 =$

120. $(5^2) \times (7^2) + 7 =$

121. $(2 + 7) \times (7 + 4) =$

122. $9 + 10 - 1 + 1 =$

Mixed Numbers and Improper Fractions

Mixed numbers and improper fractions are two different ways to represent the same value of a fraction.

1. **Mixed Number:** A mixed number is a combination of a whole number and a proper fraction. For example, $2\frac{1}{3}$ is a mixed number, where 2 is the whole number part and $\frac{1}{3}$ is the fraction part.

2. **Improper Fraction:** An improper fraction is a fraction where the numerator is greater than or equal to the denominator. For example, $\frac{7}{3}$ is an improper fraction because 6 is greater than 3.

To convert a mixed number to an improper fraction, you multiply the whole number by the denominator of the fraction, add the numerator, and then write the result over the original denominator. For example:

$$2\frac{1}{3} = \frac{2 \times 3 + 1}{3} = \frac{7}{3}$$

To convert an improper fraction to a mixed number, we divide the numerator by the denominator. The quotient becomes the whole number part, and the remainder becomes the numerator of the fraction. For example:

$$\frac{7}{3} = 2\frac{1}{3}$$

Mixed Numbers: Addition and Subtraction

To add or subtract mixed numbers, we follow similar steps as when adding or subtracting regular fractions. For instance:

Addition:

- Add the whole numbers: Add the whole number parts of the mixed numbers together.
- Add the fractions: Add the fractions parts of the mixed numbers together.
- Simplify (if needed): If the fraction part of the sum is an improper fraction, simplify it by converting it to a mixed number.

Subtraction:

- Subtract the whole numbers: Subtract the whole number part of the second mixed number from the whole number part of the first mixed number.
- Subtract the fractions: Subtract the fraction part of the second mixed number from the fraction part of the first mixed number.
- Simplify (if needed): If the fraction part of the difference is a negative fraction, borrow from the whole number part or simplify it by converting it to a mixed number.

Mixed Numbers: Multiplication and Division

To multiply or divide mixed numbers, we follow these steps:

Multiplication:

- <u>Convert the mixed numbers to improper fractions:</u> Multiply the whole number by the denominator of the fraction, then add the numerator. Write the result over the original denominator.
- <u>Multiply the fractions:</u> Multiply the numerators together to get the new numerator and multiply the denominators together to get the new denominator.
- <u>Simplify (if needed):</u> If the result is an improper fraction, simplify it by converting it back to a mixed number.

Division:

- <u>Convert the mixed numbers to improper fractions:</u>
- <u>Invert the divisor:</u> Flip the second fraction (the one you're dividing by) so that the division becomes multiplication.
- <u>Multiply the fractions:</u> Multiply the numerators together to get the new numerator and multiply the denominators together to get the new denominator.
- <u>Simplify (if needed):</u> If the result is an improper fraction, simplify it by converting it back to a mixed number.

Multiplication with whole numbers

To multiply a fraction by a whole number, we simply multiply the numerator of the fraction by the whole number while keeping the denominator the same.

For example, if we have $\frac{2}{3}$ and we want to multiply it by 5:

$$5 \times \frac{2}{3} = \frac{5 \times 2}{3} = \frac{10}{3}$$

Mixed Numbers

Calculate.

123. $6\frac{7}{10} - 3\frac{2}{3} =$ _______________

124. $3\frac{4}{8} + 8\frac{3}{6} =$ _______________

125. $5\frac{4}{5} \times 6\frac{1}{2} =$ _______________

126. $3\frac{6}{7} \times 8\frac{8}{9} =$ _______________

127. $3\frac{1}{4} + 7\frac{1}{2} =$ _______________

128. $9\frac{1}{3} - 2\frac{2}{5} =$ _______________________

129. $9\frac{3}{6} \times 5\frac{2}{4} =$ _______________________

130. $8\frac{2}{8} + 5\frac{6}{10} =$ _______________________

131. $9\frac{1}{9} - 7\frac{2}{7} =$ _______________________

132. $8\frac{2}{5} \div 8\frac{5}{6} =$ _______________________

133. $6\frac{3}{4} - 4\frac{3}{8} =$ _______________

134. $9\frac{3}{10} \div 8\frac{1}{2} =$ _______________

135. $7\frac{2}{7} + 9\frac{1}{3} =$ _______________

136. $2\frac{1}{9} \times 6\frac{3}{6} =$ _______________

137. $3\frac{5}{7} + 3\frac{7}{10} =$ _______________

138. $4\frac{2}{3} + 2\frac{1}{5} =$ _______________________________

139. $5\frac{1}{8} - 4\frac{2}{4} =$ _______________________________

140. $7\frac{1}{2} \times 6\frac{5}{9} =$ _______________________________

141. $3\frac{1}{6} \times 5\frac{3}{4} =$ _______________________________

142. $2\frac{5}{10} + 9\frac{1}{8} =$ _______________________________

143. $3\frac{4}{7} \div 2\frac{8}{9} =$ ________________

144. $3\frac{1}{2} + 7\frac{1}{3} =$ ________________

145. $8\frac{1}{5} \div 7\frac{5}{9} =$ ________________

146. $1\frac{1}{2} + 7\frac{3}{10} =$ ________________

147. $9\frac{5}{6} - 7\frac{5}{8} =$ ________________

148. $8\frac{3}{5} + 9\frac{1}{7} =$ ________________________

149. $8\frac{1}{3} \div 6\frac{3}{4} =$ ________________________

150. $6\frac{2}{10} - 5\frac{2}{4} =$ ________________________

151. $7\frac{2}{5} \div 6\frac{2}{7} =$ ________________________

152. $5\frac{6}{9} \times 7\frac{1}{2} =$ ________________________

SUMMER ALGEBRA WORKBOOK

BUILDING ACTIVITIES

Equations (One Side)

Solve for the variable.

153. $y - 5 = 12$

154. $z - 10 = 1$

155. $19 + x = 24$

156. $11z + 6 = 226$

157. $18 - 2z = 8$

158. $3 + 8z = 123$

159. $9z + 10 = 91$

160. $k \div 8 = 6$

161. $4 \times x = 64$

162. $m \div 11 = 7$

163. $2 + z = 22$

164. $7k - 20 = 57$

165. $10 - x = 8$

166. $x \times 14 = 280$

167. $10 \times k = 40$

168. $z + 2 = 5$

169. $8y + 8 = 104$

170. $m \times 14 = 84$

171. $k + 4 = 6$

172. $k + 19 = 33$

173. $9 - m = 7$

174. $80 \div k = 10$

175. $17 \div x = 1$

176. $17 \times x = 323$

177. $6 - y = 3$

178. $m \times 4 = 72$

179. $288 \div x = 18$

180. $10 + 12y = 166$

181. $222 - 20x = 2$

182. $8 + 5x = 53$

183. $17 - x = 13$

184. $m - 10 = 8$

185. $k \div 3 = 12$

186. $67 - 16z = 3$

187. $z \div 3 = 11$

188. $y \times 6 = 6$

189. $k \div 20 = 7$

190. $19 - y = 11$

191. $y - 8 = 2$

192. $m + 11 = 12$

193. $z - 15 = 1$

194. $y \times 15 = 225$

195. $1 \times m = 19$

196. $18k - 1 = 17$

197. $y - 12 = 5$

198. $3z + 17 = 44$

199. $14 + z = 32$

200. $12 + 12z = 120$

201. $z \div 16 = 15$

202. $18m + 15 = 249$

Solving Inequalities

Inequalities are mathematical expressions that compare the relative sizes of two values. They are used to express relationships where one quantity is:

- "$<$" (less than),
- "$>$" (greater than),
- "$<=$" (less than or equal to),
- "$>=$" (greater than or equal to),
- and "$\neq$" (not equal to) another quantity.

For example:

$$y + \text{-}10 \leq \text{-}8$$

To isolate y, we need to get rid of the constant term -10. Since -10 is being subtracted from y, we can undo this operation by adding 10 to both sides of the inequality:

$$y - 10 + 10 \leq -8 + 10$$

$$y \leq 2$$

To check the solution:

$$2 - 10 \leq -8$$

$$-8 = -8$$

The inequality is true when $y = 2$

Solving Inequalities

203.

$$-5 \leq m + 9$$

204.

$$-2 \leq -3z$$

205.

$$\frac{z}{-8} > 7$$

206.

$$2 - x \leq 4$$

207.
$$-7 - m \geq -2$$

208.
$$7 > -4 + z$$

209.
$$12\,m \geq -6$$

210.
$$5 \leq \frac{m}{-5}$$

211.

$$-9 < \frac{y}{-2}$$

212.

$$-8 < -16x$$

213.

$$-1 - z > 1$$

214.

$$-3 \leq k + 2$$

215.

$$5 - x > 7$$

216.

$$-12 \geq 18\,y$$

217.

$$\frac{y}{5} \leq 7$$

218.

$$9 < -6 + m$$

219.

$$-12 < -9\,m$$

220.

$$5 \geq y + 6$$

221.

$$2 > -9 - m$$

222.

$$5 \geq \frac{m}{-7}$$

223.

$$9 < -2 + x$$

224.

$$-2x < -10$$

225.

$$-3 - z > 9$$

226.

$$3 \leq \frac{z}{2}$$

227.

$$\frac{x}{1} \le -5$$

228.

$$y - 5 < 9$$

229.

$$k + -7 \le 5$$

230.

$$-2 \ge 6x$$

231.

$$m - -7 \leq -2$$

232.

$$-3 < -6 + x$$

233.

$$-6\,y \leq 5$$

234.

$$\frac{m}{-3} \leq -5$$

Evaluate Expressions

Evaluating expressions involves substituting given values for variables in an expression and then performing the indicated operations to find the result.

For example: Let's evaluate $4x - 10$, when $x = 3$:

Step 1: Substitute the given value for the variable:

Replace every occurrence of x in the expression $4x - 10$ with the given value, which is 3:

$$= 4(3) - 10$$

Step 2: Perform the operations:

Perform the indicated operations according to the order of operations (PEMDAS - Parentheses, Exponents, Multiplication and Division, Addition and Subtraction):

$$= 4 \times 3 - 10$$

Step 3: Simplify:

Calculate the result:

$$12 - 10 = 2$$

Evaluate Equations

Evaluate each expression when: x = 2

235. $(x)^1 =$

236. $3(4 - x) =$

237. $8(8 + x) =$

238. $9x + 8 =$

239. $4x + 4 =$

240. $x^1 + x - 2 =$

241. $1 + x =$

242. $x \div 1 =$

243. $x + 10 =$

244. $2x + 7 + (9x - 9) =$

Evaluate Equations

Evaluate each expression when: $x = 5$

245. $10(4 + x) =$

246. $3(4 - x) =$

247. $9(7 - x) =$

248. $x - 2 =$

249. $9 + x =$

250. $5 \div x + 2 =$

251. $4x + x =$

252. $x - 9 =$

253. $x - 5 =$

254. $1 + x =$

Evaluate Equations

Evaluate each expression when: $x = 4$

255. $10x + 3 =$

256. $9 + (10x + 7) =$

257. $8 \div x =$

258. $5x + 5 =$

259. $2(3x) =$

260. $4 \div x =$

261. $8x + 8 - 6x =$

262. $5x^1 + 7x^1 =$

263. $x(5 + x) =$

264. $4 \div x =$

Evaluate Equations

Evaluate each expression when: $x = 4$

265. $3x + 5 - 3x =$

266. $(8x)^1 =$

267. $10x + 3 + (4x - 3) =$

268. $9(2x) =$

269. $8(10 - x) =$

270. $x + 5 =$

271. $x - 8 =$

272. $x + 6 =$

273. $\dfrac{x}{1} + 6 =$

274. $10 - x =$

Evaluate Equations

Evaluate each expression when: $x = 6$

275. $9x + 5 + (7x - 8) =$

276. $(x + 9) \div 1 =$

277. $4x + 9x - 2 =$

278. $6 \div x =$

279. $(5x + 10) + (4x - 5) =$

280. $(9x + 5) + (4x - 8) =$

281. $4x - 8 =$

282. $6x - 7 + 7x =$

283. $10(7 - x) =$

284. $8x + 4 =$

Percentage

Percentage is a way of expressing a number as a fraction of 100. It is commonly used to represent proportions, rates, and comparisons. The symbol "%" is used to denote percentages.

To calculate a percentage, we multiply the given number by the appropriate fraction or decimal equivalent.

How to calculate a percentage:

Convert Percentage to Decimal: If the percentage is given as a percentage value (e.g., 25%), convert it to its decimal equivalent by dividing by 100.

$$\text{For example, 25\% as a decimal is } \frac{25}{100} = 0.25$$

Multiply: Multiply the decimal equivalent of the percentage by the given number. This gives us the portion of the number that represents the percentage.

$$100 \times 0.25 = 25\%$$

Result: The result is the calculated percentage value.

For example, to calculate 25% of 80:

Convert 25% to a decimal: 25% = 0.25.

Multiply 0.25 by 80: $0.25 \times 80 = 20$. The result is 20.

Percent Word Problems

Percent word problems involve situations where percentages are used to calculate quantities or amounts. These problems often require converting percentages to decimals and then applying them to the given values.

For example:

Bella bought a pair of shoes for $90.00. If she paid an additional 90% for taxes, how much in total did she pay for the shoes?

- Bella bought a pair of shoes for $90.00.
- She paid an additional 90% for taxes.

Calculate 90% of $90:

Tax= 90% × 90

Tax= 0.90 × 90

Tax= $81

Add the tax amount to the original price:

Total cost= $90 + $81

Total cost= $171

Percentage

Find the percentage of given numbers.

285. 60% of 500 = ☐

286. 50% of 700 = ☐

287. 15% of 80 = ☐

288. ☐ of 600 = 1800

289. ☐ of 400 = 300

290. ☐ of 800 = 16

291. ☐ of 500 = 50

292. 80% of ☐ = 560

293. 30% of 600 = ☐

294. ☐ of 100 = 6

295. ☐ of 70 = 17.5

296. ☐ of 900 = 81

297. 1% of 400 = ☐

298. 15% of ☐ = 120

299. ☐ of 900 = 270

300. 70% of 700 = ☐

301. ☐ of 200 = 160

302. 7% of ☐ = 49

303. 4% of ☐ = 1.2

304. 3% of ☐ = 15

305. 60% of $100 = $ ☐

306. ☐ of $800 = 2400$

307. ☐ of $500 = 200$

308. 200% of ☐ $= 1000$

309. ☐ of $200 = 150$

310. ☐ of $500 = 5$

311. 25% of ☐ $= 25$

312. 100% of $500 = $ ☐

313. 35% of $900 = $ ☐

314. 8% of ☐ $= 56$

315. 6% of ⬚ = 30

316. 9% of 100 = ⬚

317. 20% of 50 = ⬚

318. 10% of ⬚ = 90

319. 90% of ⬚ = 630

320. 5% of ⬚ = 20

321. 50% of ⬚ = 10

322. 25% of ⬚ = 200

323. ⬚ of 400 = 16

324. 1% of ⬚ = 0.7

325. [ ] of 300 = 60

326. [ ] of 400 = 1200

327. [ ] of 800 = 720

328. [ ] of 700 = 210

329. [ ] of 900 = 72

330. 70% of [ ] = 350

331. 200% of [ ] = 600

332. [ ] of 800 = 48

333. [ ] of 200 = 120

334. 50% of 90 = [ ]

Percent Word Problems

335. Nicholas bought a bicycle that cost $60.00 when it was new. If he eventually sold it for 5% of the original cost, how much was it sold for?

336. Joshua's monthly sales of needles was $50.00. If he earned 86% of profit, what was his profit?

337. In a survey of 50 people, 8% said they preferred android OS. How many people preferred android OS?

338. Jackson buys bags for $75.00 to sell them in market. If he wants to earn 4% profit. What must be the selling price of bags?

339. Trinity had a collection of 25 baseball cards. She gave away 4% of them. How many did she have left?

340. Levi earned $100.00 for a week's work. If he paid 33% of it in taxes how much did he pay in taxes?

341. A store has 100 thermometers. If 93% of them are sold at the end of the day, how many thermometers are sold?

342. In a class of 75 students, 84% of them are in the Math Club. How many students are in the Math Club?

343. In a class of 80 students, 5% are girls. How many are girls?

344. Sebastian had 20 flosses. He gave away 35% of them. How many did he have left?

345. If the number 50 is decreased by 4%, what is the value of the new number?

346. What is 8% of 25?

347. A store offers 15% discount on all products. If the original price of bats was 80, what is the sales price?

348. A store offers a 34% discount on all items. If Hailey buys gloves originally priced at $50.00, how much money did she save?

349. A restaurant makes a pizza that is 60 inches in diameter. If they want to increase the size of the pizza by 5%, what will be the new diameter?

350. In a class of 40 students, 5% are boys. How many are boys?

351. Bella bought a camera for $50.00. If she paid an additional 84% for sales tax, how much in total did she pay for the camera?

352. Emma bought thermometers for $50.00. If she paid an additional 4% for sales tax, how much in total did she pay for the thermometers?

353. Emilia bought a pizza for $50.00. If she paid an additional 6% for sales tax, how much in total did she pay for the pizza?

354. A store offers 5% discount on all products. If the sale price of plates was 60, what was the original price?

<u>**Ratio and Proportion**</u>

A proportional relationship between two quantities exists when they have a constant ratio or when one is a multiple of the other. In other words, if we increase one quantity, the other quantity will increase or decrease by the same factor. For example, if we double one quantity, the other quantity will also double.

Let's solve a problem:

$$\frac{\square}{9} = \frac{8}{18}$$

Step 1: Cross Multiply: Cross multiply by multiplying the numerator of one fraction by the denominator of the other, and vice versa:

$$x \times 18 = 9 \times 8$$

Step 2: Solve for the Unknown: Perform the multiplication on both sides of the equation:

$$18x = 72$$

Step 3: Divide Both Sides by the Coefficient of the Unknown: To isolate x, divide both sides of the equation by the coefficient of x, which is 18:

$$\frac{18x}{18} = \frac{72}{18}$$

$$x = 4$$

Step 4: Verify Check your solution by substituting x = 4 back into the original equation:

$$\frac{4}{9} = \frac{8}{18}$$

Since both sides are equal, the solution x = 4 is correct.

Ratio and Proportion Word Problems

We can use the concept of proportionality in solving many word problems, for example:

If a car travels 620 miles in six hours, how far can it travel in 12 hours?

Since the car travels a certain distance in a certain amount of time, we can assume that the distance traveled is directly proportional to the time taken.

Let d be the distance the car can travel in 12 hours.

We can set up a proportion:

$$\frac{\text{Distance1}}{\text{Time1}} = \frac{\text{Distance2}}{\text{Time2}}$$

Substituting the given values:

$$\frac{620 \text{ miles}}{6 \text{ hours}} = \frac{d}{12 \text{ hours}}$$

Now, let's solve for d:

$$d = \frac{620 \times 12}{6} = \frac{7440}{6} = 1240$$

So, the car can travel 1240 miles in 12 hours.

Ratio and Proportion Word Problems

355. Sebastian drives 200 miles in four hours. How far can he travel in 10 hours?

356. If five workers can build a wall in 17 hours, how many workers are needed to build the wall in seven hours?

357. If a square has an area of 69 square meters, what is the length of each side of the square?

358. If a car travels 561 miles in four hours, how far can it travel in 12 hours?

359. A recipe calls for four cups of sugar for every nine cups of flour. If you have 12 cups of flour, how much sugar is needed?

360. If six workers can complete a job in 19 days, how many workers are needed to complete the job in eight days?

361. If a map scale is 1 inch to five miles, how far apart are two cities that are nine inches apart on the map?

362. If a recipe calls for three cups of water for every five cups of rice, how much water is needed for eight cups of rice?

363. A road is 97 miles long and it takes a car three hour to travel the entire length. What is the speed of the car in miles per hour?

364. A zoo has a ratio of three monkeys to every 10 lions. If there are 46 lions in the zoo, how many monkeys are there?

365. A charity received a donation of $2,224 from a company. If the donation was divided among five charities in the ratio 2:3:4:5:6, how much did the third charity receive?

366. If a recipe calls for three eggs for every eight cups of flour, how many eggs are needed for 18 cups of flour?

367. If it takes three students 15 hours to complete a science project, how many students are needed to finish the project in six hours?

368. A charity received a donation of $1,630 from a company. If the donation was divided among five charities in the ratio 2:3:4:5:6, how much did the fourth charity receive?

369. A train travels 297 miles in four hours. How far can it travel in seven hours?

370. A room has an area of 134 square meters and a length of 19 meters. What is the width of the room?

371. If 10 chefs can bake 100 cakes in 19 hours, how many chefs are needed to bake the same number of cakes in eight hours?

372. A company has a ratio of four managers for every 24 employees. If the company has 161 employees, how many managers are there?

373. A farmer has a ratio of four sheep to every eight cows in his pasture. If there are 48 cows in the pasture, how many sheep are there?

374. A school has a teacher-student ratio of 1:20. If there are 818 students, how many teachers are needed?

375. A car can travel 43 miles per gallon of gas. How many gallons of gas are needed to travel 174 miles?

ANSWERS

Page 1: Exponents

1. 1/144	**2.** 1/361	**3.** 50,625	**4.** 289	**5.** 1/9	**6.** 1/81
7. 144	**8.** 512	**9.** 1/3375	**10.** 25	**11.** 1/49	**12.** 49
13. 100	**14.** 1/36	**15.** 64	**16.** 1/125	**17.** 38,416	**18.** 1/256
19. 400	**20.** 125	**21.** 1/64	**22.** 1/4	**23.** 1/8000	**24.** 1/216
25. 1/64	**26.** 1/121	**27.** 1/25	**28.** 256	**29.** 6,859	**30.** 196
31. 27	**32.** 1/4913	**33.** 9	**34.** 1/5832		

Page 4: Square and Cube Roots

35. 4	**36.** 7	**37.** 1	**38.** 2	**39.** 17	**40.** 2	**41.** 7	**42.** 9	**43.** 9
44. 7	**45.** 16	**46.** 27	**47.** 11	**48.** 4	**49.** 2	**50.** 3	**51.** 3	**52.** 1
53. 5	**54.** 6	**55.** 17	**56.** 13	**57.** 1	**58.** 84	**59.** 83	**60.** 30	**61.** 69
62. 5	**63.** 9	**64.** 10						

Page 7: Multiple Operations Fractions

65. 1 9/20	**66.** 1 13/20	**67.** 1 7/40	**68.** 25/28	**69.** 7/10
70. 55/126	**71.** 1 1/45	**72.** 151/315	**73.** 6 3/5	**74.** 1 23/120
75. 1 7/50	**76.** 25/27	**77.** 19/45	**78.** 1/3	**79.** 1 37/150
80. 2 193/360	**81.** 13/20	**82.** 1/30		

Page 11: Order of Operations (PEMDAS)

83. 42	**84.** 36	**85.** 238	**86.** 19	**87.** 4	**88.** 108
89. 21	**90.** 16	**91.** 10	**92.** 17	**93.** 80	**94.** 13
95. 20	**96.** 144	**97.** 100	**98.** 450	**99.** 5	**100.** 233

101. 2,034 **102.** 36 **103.** 44 **104.** 232 **105.** 1.4 **106.** 107

107. 69 **108.** 10 **109.** 7 **110.** 14 **111.** 164 **112.** 1.8

113. 81 **114.** 33 **115.** 15 **116.** 100 **117.** 18 **118.** 280

119. 24 **120.** 1,232 **121.** 99 **122.** 19

Page 16:   Mixed Numbers

123. 3 1/30 **124.** 12 **125.** 37 7/10 **126.** 34 2/7 **127.** 10 3/4

128. 6 14/15 **129.** 52 1/4 **130.** 13 17/20 **131.** 1 52/63 **132.** 252/265

133. 2 3/8 **134.** 1 8/85 **135.** 16 13/21 **136.** 13 13/18 **137.** 7 29/70

138. 6 13/15 **139.** 5/8 **140.** 49 1/6 **141.** 18 5/24 **142.** 11 5/8

143. 1 43/182 **144.** 10 5/6 **145.** 1 29/340 **146.** 8 4/5 **147.** 2 5/24

148. 17 26/35 **149.** 1 19/81 **150.** 7/10 **151.** 1 39/220 **152.** 42 1/2

Page 22:   Equations (One Side)

153. y = 17 **154.** z = 11 **155.** x = 5 **156.** z = 20 **157.** z = 5

158. z = 15 **159.** z = 9 **160.** k = 48 **161.** x = 16 **162.** m = 77

163. z = 20 **164.** k = 11 **165.** x = 2 **166.** x = 20 **167.** k = 4

168. z = 3 **169.** y = 12 **170.** m = 6 **171.** k = 2 **172.** k = 14

173. m = 2 **174.** k = 8 **175.** x = 17 **176.** x = 19 **177.** y = 3

178. m = 18 **179.** x = 16 **180.** y = 13 **181.** x = 11 **182.** x = 9

183. x = 4 **184.** m = 18 **185.** k = 36 **186.** z = 4 **187.** z = 33

188. y = 1 **189.** k = 140 **190.** y = 8 **191.** y = 10 **192.** m = 1

193. z = 16 **194.** y = 15 **195.** m = 19 **196.** k = 1 **197.** y = 17

198. z = 9 **199.** z = 18 **200.** z = 9 **201.** z = 240 **202.** m = 13

Page 27: Solving Inequalities

203. m ≥ -14   **204.** z ≥ 2/3   **205.** z > -56   **206.** x ≤ -2   **207.** m ≥ -5

208. z < 11   **209.** m ≥ -1/2   **210.** m ≥ -25   **211.** y > 18   **212.** x > 1/2

213. z > -2   **214.** k ≥ -5   **215.** x > -2   **216.** y ≤ -2/3   **217.** y ≤ 35

218. m > 15   **219.** m > 4/3   **220.** y ≤ -1   **221.** m < -11   **222.** m ≤ -35

223. x > 11   **224.** x < 5   **225.** z > -12   **226.** z ≥ 6   **227.** x ≤ -5

228. y < 14   **229.** k ≤ 12   **230.** x ≤ -1/3   **231.** m ≤ -9   **232.** x > 3

233. y ≤ -5/6   **234.** m ≤ 15

Page 35: Evaluate Equations

235. 2   **236.** 6   **237.** 80   **238.** 26   **239.** 12   **240.** 2   **241.** 3   **242.** 2

243. 12   **244.** 20

Page 36: Evaluate Equations

245. 90   **246.** -3   **247.** 18   **248.** 3   **249.** 14   **250.** 3   **251.** 25   **252.** -4

253. 0   **254.** 6

Page 37: Evaluate Equations

255. 43   **256.** 56   **257.** 2   **258.** 25   **259.** 24   **260.** 1   **261.** 16   **262.** 48

263. 36   **264.** 1

Page 38: Evaluate Equations

265. 5   **266.** 32   **267.** 56   **268.** 72   **269.** 48   **270.** 9   **271.** -4   **272.** 10

273. 10   **274.** 6

Page 39: Evaluate Equations

275. 93   **276.** 15   **277.** 76   **278.** 1   **279.** 59   **280.** 75   **281.** 16   **282.** 71

283. 10   **284.** 52

Page 40: Percentage

285. 300   **286.** 350   **287.** 12   **288.** 300%   **289.** 75%   **290.** 2%

291. 10%   **292.** 700   **293.** 180   **294.** 6%   **295.** 25%   **296.** 9%

297. 4   **298.** 800   **299.** 30%   **300.** 490   **301.** 80%   **302.** 700

303. 30   **304.** 500   **305.** 60   **306.** 300%   **307.** 40%   **308.** 500

309. 75%   **310.** 1%   **311.** 100   **312.** 500   **313.** 315   **314.** 700

315. 500   **316.** 9   **317.** 10   **318.** 900   **319.** 700   **320.** 400

321. 20   **322.** 800   **323.** 4%   **324.** 70   **325.** 20%   **326.** 300%

327. 90%   **328.** 30%   **329.** 8%   **330.** 500   **331.** 300   **332.** 6%

333. 60%   **334.** 45

Page 45: Percent Word Problems

335. $3.00   **336.** $43.00   **337.** 4   **338.** $78.00   **339.** 24

340. $33.00   **341.** 93   **342.** 63   **343.** 4   **344.** 13

345. 48   **346.** 2   **347.** 68   **348.** $17.00   **349.** 63

350. 2   **351.** $92.00   **352.** $52.00   **353.** $53.00   **354.** 63

Page 50: Ratio and Proportion Word Problems

355. 500   **356.** 12.14   **357.** 8.31   **358.** 1,683   **359.** 5.33

360. 14.25   **361.** 45   **362.** 4.8   **363.** 32.33   **364.** 13.8

365. 444.8   **366.** 6.75   **367.** 7.5   **368.** 407.5   **369.** 519.75

370. 7.05   **371.** 23.75   **372.** 26.83   **373.** 24   **374.** 40.9

375. 4.05

www.ingramcontent.com/pod-product-compliance
Lightning Source LLC
Chambersburg PA
CBHW081952160726
47999CB00008B/2600